TALES OF THE CARIBBEAN: A MEMOIR:

BOOK 2
MY LIFE AS A MISSIONARY

AUTHOR: ISABELLA L- CLARKE

Scripture quotations marked KJV are from the Holy
Bible, King James Version (Authorized Version).
First published in 1611. Quoted from the KJV Classic
Reference Bible, Copyright © 1983 by The Zondervan
Corporation.

To order additional copies of this book, contact:
Xlibris
1-888-795-4274
www.Xlibris.com
Orders@Xlibris.com

ISBN: Softcover   978-1-4990-6805-4
        EBook   978-1-4990-6804-7

Print information available on the last page

Rev. date: 06/09/2020

DEDICATION

This book is dedicated in loving memory of my parents, Mr. & Mrs. Walter and Rosalie Pollard who, through their teaching in my upbringing and the life that they lived, helped to prepare me for the mission field.

It is also dedicated to missionaries both domestic and international, hoping that in reading the contents of this book, it will help them to identify their calling in life and help them in their ministry.

ACKNOWLEDGEMENTS

I would like to acknowledge my two children, Dr. Walter N. Lumsby and my daughter Laurianne E. Lumsby who encouraged me to write. They both said that I have a lot of knowledge and history in my head and that I need to write books about it.

I would also like to acknowledge Sister Tracia who has been an inspiration and consultant to me in my writings.

WHO IS ISABELLA L-CLARKE?

Who is Isabella L-Clarke? She is the daughter of Mr. & Mrs. Walter and Rosalie Pollard. She was born in the island of Barbados, West Indies in the 1940's. She obtained her spiritual teaching at the St. Bartholomew's Anglican Church where she attended church services and Sunday School regularly. It was there where she developed her prayer life and the teaching to, "Help others first and self last." She observed how the leaders of the different auxiliaries in the church prepared and served the elderly people who were sick and shut in, especially at Christmas time, Easter, and Harvest time. During the week day service, the Priest also visited the sick and shut in, and took and served them Holy Communion.

While attending the St. Bartholomew's Girls' Elementary School, she was also taught to memorize some of the Holy Scriptures, some hymns, and prayers. There she continued to develop her spiritual education as well as her academic education. The priest also came to the school to check and to see how his Sunday School students were doing.

After coming to America and serving as a missionary for many years, she was ordained as an evangelist. Being diligent in her ministry, she was later ordained as an Elder in the church where she is now an active member in New York City. She travels back and forth to Barbados on many occasions to continue her missionary work there. Her greatest concern is winning souls to Christ. She is also focused on encouraging children and young adults to stay in school, acquire a good education, and get a good job before taking on the greater responsibilities of adult life. She also has greatest respect for the senior citizens, and tries to assist and encourage them in any way she can.

Isabella L-Clarke is also a seamstress, using her skills to help others. She is a mother of three children, a grandmother of five, a great grandmother of eight, and a great, great, grandmother of one. She is a retired teacher who worked for 22 years with children who had special needs, and sometimes with children in general education. Before that, she worked for many years with children in early childhood education.

Contents

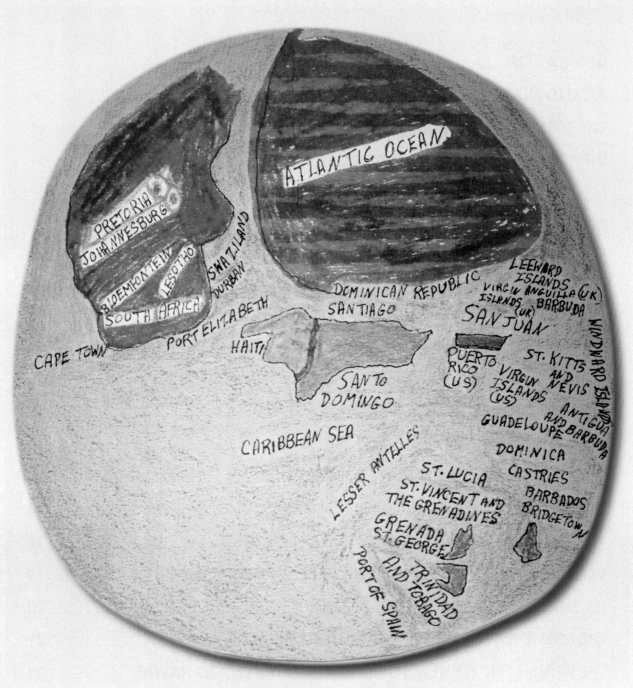

This Map Represents Some Of The Places
Where Missionary Isabella L-Clarke Traveled.

INTRODUCTION TO THE GARDEN OF PRAYER MINISTRY

The Garden of Prayer is a name recently given to a ministry which began in 1972. On June 19, 1961, I left the district of Charnocks, Christ Church, in the Island of Barbados, West Indies, to visit my aunt Albertina in the United States of America. She lived in New York City.

Being born and raised in the village of Sea View, Christ Church, I often walked through the district of Fairy Valley, Christ Church, to attend the St. Bartholomew's Girls' Elementary School. I noticed that there were many children living there whose parents mostly worked on the Fairy Valley Plantation. I also noticed how the workers were being treated on the plantation and how hard they worked in the hot sun. I wished that I could help them.

After relocating to Charnocks, Christ Church, with my family at the age of 16 years old, I continued to care for my great uncle who was a senior citizen. His wife had recently died. The agreement was made by some of my family members that I would inherit a piece of his land when he died.

MY JOURNEY TO AMERICA

After leaving for New York City, my mother took over the responsibility of caring for her uncle. As the airplane rose over the Island of Barbados that day, I looked over the Island especially the district of Fairy Valley, and promised God that I would reach back and help my people there. During the month of March 1962, while I was still in New York City, my great uncle died. He left in his Will, a portion of land to be divided between my mother and me.

During the time between 1962 and 1971, I became married to Mr. Joseph Lumsby. Together, we raised our two children, Lucille and Walter. During that time after the birth of our son, Walter, my husband became ill. Sometimes he was admitted into the hospital and sometimes he was sick at home. After being readmitted into the hospital one year, he seemed to be angry because he was sick. There were times when I visited him when he began fussing at me for no reason. I was then known as Mrs. Isabella Lumsby. I did not like him fussing at me. One day I told him that if he continued to fuss at me, I would go and visit some of the other patients who may appreciate me visiting them, and so I did. As I walked through the hospital wards looking at the other patients, I noticed some of them were being treated with medication intravenously. The feeding tube was connected to the arm of the patient and then connected to a tall metal pole. At the bottom of the pole was very heavy but it was on wheels. Wherever the patient wanted to go, he had to pull that heavy pole along with him. As I looked at other patients just laying there in their beds, it was then that I said, "Lord, these people are like sheep just waiting to die. It should be something better for them than this." It was then that I began visiting the patients.

THE BEGINNING OF My MINISTRY

I had been attending an Episcopal Church since I came to America. It was the same teaching as the Anglican Church in Barbados. After obtaining a job in a Church of God In Christ, Day Care Center, I became a member of that church. Since it was noticed that I had much love and compassion for people and for the children whom I cared for, I was told that I was a missionary. I responded by saying that I thought a missionary was one who went around spreading the gospel of Jesus Christ. I was told that spreading the gospel of Jesus Christ was also part of being a missionary. I was then taught by the pastor and the missionaries of that church how to present myself as a missionary. Because of the difference in denomination, my husband, at that time did not accept the fact that I was a missionary.

I was then brought before the church's District Missionary Board and questioned by the head of the District Missionary Department before being given a missionary license. From that time on, if there was any person whom the pastor knew was sick, he would ask the missionaries to visit them whether in the hospital, in their home, or in a nursing home. The pastor suggested that we wear a white uniform when going on the mission field.

When going into the hospital he wanted us to wear a nurse's hat. Since I had taken a course in Nursing Assistant, Baby and Geriatric Care, I had a nurse's hat. I was even chosen to visit city officials in the hospital, who were connected to the day care program. It was also recommended that I became a member of a community board at one of the community hospitals in the neighborhood. Since I was exposed to the community in such a way, I was then able to volunteer my services in the hospitals and nursing homes. I was able to plan services with the head worker in the volunteer department.

During the Christmas season, I went around to stores asking for donations of toys and clothing for children in the hospitals and for clothing for the adults. Some of the managers of the stores gave me toys and some said that I could purchase some at a discount price. Sometimes I received donations of clothing from parents who worked in factories. When a clothing line was discontinued, their boss gave them the clothes that were left over. They brought them to the day care center and gave them to me, telling me that they were to be taken to the children overseas. Parents also donated used clothing which their children outgrew. These clothing were still in good condition. They also said that the clothes were to be sent or taken to the children overseas as well.

In explaining all of this, I want you to know that I, as well as others, recognized the calling of God upon my life and the anointing of His Holy Spirit upon me as I began to submit myself to His calling.

After observing the conditions of the patients in the hospital as I visited my husband, I spoke with some of them and prayed for them as they requested prayer. I returned to my husband's bedside and began to pray for him. He asked me to pray aloud. I closed my eyes and began to pray aloud. The anointing of God fell upon me as I prayed. When the Spirit of God lifted from me and I opened my eyes, I realized that many nurses and doctors were standing around me. They asked me at which hospital did I work. They did not recognize me as one of their staff. They thought that I came to substitute for another nurse who was absent. I told them that I was not a nurse but that I was a missionary visiting the sick and that my husband was there in the hospital. I showed them where he was. It was then that my husband acknowledged me as a missionary.

Next to my husband's bedside, there was another patient lying in his bed. He could not walk. He began to talk to me. He told me that he was a backslider. He said how he worshipped God but then he backslid. He said how he had gangrene in his feet and the doctors had to amputate one of his feet. He began to sing a hymn, "Lord I'm coming home. I have wandered far away from God now I'm coming home never more to roam." He requested for me to sing the hymn with him. I realized that through my praying for my husband and the other patients in the ward that this one man felt convicted of his sins. He repented of his sins and was asking God, on his bed of sickness, to open wide His arms of love because he was coming back home to God.

After the death of my husband, I developed a system where I took most of my salary, at that time, to purchase Avon products to take to the hospitals and nursing homes to distribute to those who were sick. I made sure that I took care of my children first and then explained to them that I had to go on a mission to the nursing home or hospital to visit the senior citizens. I hugged and kissed them and then I left them in God's care. My next door neighbor was informed of my leaving and she took my children to her apartment and kept them with her children until I returned home. I remembered one of the seniors asking me, upon receiving a gift of cologne, "Do you think this would make me younger when I put it on?" Another senior in the nursing home began to cry. She said that her daughter took all of her money, put her in the nursing home, and don't even come to visit her. In situations like these, you have to be very careful how you respond to them.

I informed my pastor at that time that I had a dream. In the dream, I was in Barbados in the district of Fairy Valley with other missionaries. As I was walking towards a particular house to visit someone who was sick, I noticed that the missionaries, who were supposed to be walking with me, were walking at a distance apart from me. I also discovered that, on my return, there was a group of four people in a picture which included me. One person was the tallest, the next person was a little shorter than the first, the third person was a little shorter, and the fourth person was even a little shorter than the third.

My pastor listened to what was said in the dream and then he told me to watch my friends. He said that everyone who says they are my friends, are not going to be with me. By the following Sunday afternoon, part of that dream came true. I had set up a service with the director of the volunteer department for the sick in the hospital. The director of the volunteer department said that she would not be there but she had the piano set up in an area and left someone in charge. I made arrangements with the missionaries at the church to accompany me to the hospital for the service that Sunday afternoon. After the church service was over that Sunday morning, everyone at the church had lunch. When the time came for the missionaries and the musician to go to the hospital with me, all of the missionaries, as well as the musician backed out. My mother, who lived about two and a half blocks from the church, was also invited to go along to the hospital for the service. Seeing that the group of missionaries had backed out from going to the hospital, I took my two children, met my mother around the corner and we all went to the hospital to visit the sick. We left both of the children with the security guard while we went up on the elevator to the wards. We distributed the gifts to the patients and witnessed to them. When we were finished, both my mother and I came down stairs on the elevator. We thanked the security guard for watching the children and then we left the hospital for our separate homes. Mission accomplished.

Picture of Lucille, Walter and I visiting the hospital in New York City.

That night after I went to sleep, I had another dream. This time I discovered that it was a test for me. God wanted me to know, if the missionaries did not go with me to the hospital, would I still go. God also revealed to me that the dream which I had with the four people in the picture were my mother, who was the tallest of the four, I was the second, my daughter Lucille was the third, and my son Walter was the shortest in the group of four. I began thanking God for the experience and thanking Him that I passed the test. While still in New York City, two other missionaries requested for me to accompany them as they travelled to Philadelphia witnessing to the lost souls. Sometimes they were asked to speak at other churches. Sometimes they had street meetings in front of their church in Manhattan, sometimes in the park, and sometimes on the sidewalks in Brooklyn, in certain neighborhoods. There were many other things that the Spirit of God directed me to do while I was in America.

I began to question my mother concerning the papers to my portion of the land which was willed to me by my great uncle. Instead of her giving me the information, she began to cry. I did not know what to do but to pray. One Sunday while I was in church, my assistant pastor was preaching about the widow and the unjust judge. He had spoken on that message several times before, from the book of Luke Chapter 18: verse 2-5, in the King James Version. "There was in a city a judge, which feared not God, neither regarded man: (3) and there was a widow in that city; and she came unto him, saying, Avenge me of mine adversary. (4) And he would not for a while: but afterward he said within himself, Though I fear not God, nor regard man; (5) yet because this widow troubleth me, I will avenge her, lest by her continual coming she weary me."

Normally after service, I would stay around the church and talk with the saints. This particular Sunday, the Spirit of God spoke to me and said, "When service is over, do not stop to talk with anyone but go directly over to your mother's house and give her the message that the preacher just gave." I did as the Spirit of God said.

What happened then was, my mother told me that I would have to pay a lawyer like she did. She continued by saying that she paid a lawyer to see about the land and that the lawyer took all of her money and then left the Island without doing what she paid him to do. She said that she had no way of contacting him. I was hurt.

I was only fourteen years old and just out of elementary school when I was sent to care for my great uncle. While I was in America, Uncle Robbie took sick. During his stay in the hospital, another uncle suggested to him that he should divide the pasture in his will between my mother and me because she assisted him during his sickness. My problems began when I sought to transfer my portion of the property into my name.

MY RETURN TRIP TO BARBADOS

I returned to Barbados during the summer of 1972, for the first time as a missionary. I began seeking to transfer my portion of land into my own name while I continued to do missionary work. I was told by my uncle that it would take much time and money traveling back and forth to get the property settled. After several trips to Barbados, I was referred to a lawyer. I gave him the information which I had and hired him to start working on my case. Many years went by before I was successful with the transfer. Since I had so much trouble in doing so, I made another promise to God to dedicate a portion of the land as a peace offering to Him. I promised that I would build a little mission to accommodate missionaries coming from abroad, who could not afford to pay the cost to stay at a hotel. I said that if they so desired to stay at this mission, they would pay a lower price to cover the cost of the utility and the upkeep of the building. This promise was made in the 1980's. Having difficulty with the lawyer also, the Spirit of God also told me to give him the same message about the unjust judge and the widow. After that, he began working more seriously on my papers for the land. During that time, the Barbados government cut off a large portion of the land down the hill, to build the ABC Highway, leading to the "Grantley Adams International Airport."

THE BEGINNING OF MY INTERNATIONAL MINISTRY FROM NEW YORK CITY TO BARBADOS

I started my International Ministry in 1972, after the death of my husband. I began shipping boxes of clothing, foodstuff, tracks, and Bibles to Barbados to be distributed to the people in different communities. I would arrive in Barbados about four weeks after shipping a box or a trunk, giving it enough time to arrive before I got there. On my first arrival, I brought my two children, Lucille and Walter with me.

Missionary Isabella, daughter Lucille, and son Walter on their way to Barbados, West Indies.

After having the box delivered to the guest house where we were staying in Silver Sands, Christ Church, I sent messages by Elder E. Clarke, to invite certain people from Fairy Valley, Thyme Bottom, and Charnocks, requesting for them to visit me. This is how I began my distribution.

As I looked out of the window of the guest house one morning, I saw a man staking out his sheep on a pasture near the guest house to graze. I was led to call him. He came to me and we began to talk. In recognizing that I was a missionary, he began to tell me how he believed in God and served Him. He acknowledged that he was a backslider and needed to get back to serving God. Together we prayed. He was given a Bible and some tracks. He thanked me and then he left. Every morning after that, when he brought his sheep on the pasture, he called to say Hello, to me and my two children. It was during a conversation that he discovered who I was. He realized that he was related to me through my father.

Within the next two years or so, my two children and I were joined with another missionary from another church. Elder E. Clarke, being the contact person in Barbados, notified some of the churches in Barbados when we, as missionaries would arrive. We visited other churches and then I was asked to speak at the Pilgrim Holiness church at Fairy Valley, and Pilgrim Road, in Christ Church, at Green Hill, St. Michael, and other churches. As I was sitting on the platform of the Pilgrim Holiness Church at Fairy Valley, Christ Church one night, I was about to bring the message when the Spirit of God brought to me the scripture found in Isaiah chapter 61. I read from the first verse to the fourth verse. The first verse read, "The Spirit of the Lord God is upon me; because the Lord hath anointed me to preach good tidings unto the meek; he hath sent me to bind up the brokenhearted, to proclaim liberty to the captives, and the opening of the prison to them that are bound;" It was then that I realized what my ministry in life was.

As time went on, God showed me exactly where He wanted me to go, whom I should deliver messages to, and what I should say. I went directly to my mother who lived in New York City and told her the vision. One lady living in the same building as my mother listened to the vision. She then explained to both of us that there was a church on that same spot many years ago when she was growing up. She said that the pastor in charge of the church was not living the life as a Christian should, so he died and the church went to nothing. She said that God was sending me back to Barbados, to finish the work on that same spot which the pastor had started.

On another missionary journey to Barbados, I was sent directly to the District of Fairy Valley to the same spot where I saw in the vision. It was next door to where some of my family members lived. Elder E. Clarke spoke with the pastor of The Pilgrim Holiness Church at Fairy Valley then, and told her of the vision which God showed me. The pastor made the arrangements with the congregation for the open air prayer meeting. On the evening of the meeting, everyone in the district gathered around the particular spot. Someone asked the question, "Why don't you have the meeting on this other spot?" They referred to a spot larger than where the group was standing. They said that the larger spot had more space and brighter lights. I responded to them by saying that the place where God showed me in the vision is where the Prayer Meeting must be held. I went into one of my relative's home to speak to the children and to encourage them to come outside to the prayer meeting. The Pastor noticed me speaking to the children and asked me if I knew them. I responded by saying that they were my cousins. The Pastor then said to me, "Is it not amazing that God sent you all the way from America to come to Barbados to minister to your own family?" She further went on to say that many times the church had Open-air Service but still many of the people would not come to church or give their lives to the Lord.

As the prayer meeting was about to begin, the pastor made an introduction and began to say why the prayer meeting was being held there. At that time, I announced that God had informed me to bring a special Bible to be delivered to a special person by the name of Marcia. I asked if that person was there. People answered, "Yes." They pointed to where she was standing which was on the land across the road from where the Prayer Meeting was being held. I invited Marcia to come to me in order to receive the Holy Bible and what message God gave me for her.

As the Prayer Meeting went on, everyone participated in the service. They were happy to see me and to hear what the Lord had done for me. I was Isabella, whom they all knew as a little girl growing up in Barbados. After being in America for many years, I was now returning as a missionary, preaching the Gospel of Jesus Christ. After the traditional way of opening the service with prayer, scripture reading, and the singing of songs, I was introduced as the speaker for the night. After greeting the people, I began to tell them of the vision which God showed me in a dream which caused me to return to Barbados for the open air meeting. I also said that in the vision, I saw a big cross the color of fire. The cross was over the houses, and in the area where I had to deliver the message. Then I told them how I heard a voice saying,

"Jesus has overcome the world and He is coming again." I turned to show some of the people the vision as it was occurring in the dream. Then someone in the crowd said something but I did not hear what was said. I turned to ask what was going on. In the vision, God also led me to the Holy Bible to Psalm 19 which is a Psalm of David. The first verse began, "The heavens declare the glory of God; and the firmament sheweth his handy work. (2) Day unto day uttereth speech, and night unto night sheweth knowledge." These words are found in the King James Version of the Holy Bible. As the vision went on, across the road and in the sky opposite the houses, there were many stars shining brightly. There was a flash and all of the stars disappeared. Then there was another flash and many bright shining stars reappeared with a crown full of shining bright stars. There was another flash and the bright shining stars and the crown disappeared. Another flash and the bright shining moon with many other stars surrounding it appeared. Then a voice said to me, "Tell the people of Fairy Valley that if they live right and do my Will, they will be a crown with many stars for them." As the Prayer Meeting went on, someone went to the Pastor and said something. I did not hear what was said so I asked the Pastor what was going on. The Pastor informed me that a young man walked up to her and told her that the Lord just revealed to him to claim the spot where the prayer meeting was being held and have three nights of revival there. That was the exact way that it happened in the dream. Since I had to return to New York City the next day, I was unable to witness the three nights of revival. Elder E. Clarke wrote a letter to me some time later, and reported that the three nights of revival was held on the same spot and three people were saved. As time went by, the group of missionaries grew larger.

After returning to America, there were several times that people wanted to visit America but had no place to stay. It was then I opened my home to accommodate visitors coming to America. I have accommodated: Pastors, missionaries, and family members from Barbados, Antigua, Trinidad, Canada, Dominican Republic, and India. The minister from India was in transit from California to India. He said that he was expected to meet a friend at the John F. Kennedy International Airport before he changed to another plane to go to India. He said that he rested his suitcase on the ground while waiting for his friend. He kept his foot on the suitcase but then, he took his foot off and walked away for a few seconds. When he turned around, his suitcase was gone. He said that in his suitcase was the money which he was traveling with as well as his daughter's picture. He did not know where to go. He never saw his friend. He took the Yellow Pages Telephone Directory to search for a church to ask for help. He came across the church where I was a member and called and asked for help. There was a revival going on at the time. One of the missionaries answered the phone and gave him the instructions how to get to the church. After arriving at the church, he spoke with the leaders and told them the story which I just mentioned. The leaders decided to pay for him to stay at a hotel which was across the street from the church for the night. He attended service the next night and then went back to the hotel. The church could not continue to pay for the hotel. The leaders asked me if I could accommodate him at my home and seek more information from him in order to get help for him. One of the sisters from the church was sent to stay with my children and me while he was there. I was then given the responsibility to find the Indian Embassy. After locating the address, I escorted the minister to the embassy. When they interviewed him, they told him that as long as he was living in America, there was no way that he could be stranded. He had to give the address where he was living. It appeared that he and his wife were having problems and he was trying to get back to India. He had told me that his wife died. We discovered that he had money on the bank where he lived in another state. In order for him to receive money from that bank, he had to have an account in New York City where they would transfer the money. We went to the bank where I had an account and explained to the bank manager the problem which the minister had. The bank manager in New York City had to phone the bank manager in the other state. The minister had to fill out and sign some papers in order for the money to be transferred to my account. We both had to return to the bank the next day for him to receive the money. As soon as he received the money, he booked his passage and went on to India. We were all glad that he was able to continue his journey to India.

We all thought that was the end of the problem. About six days later, I received a phone call from a woman who said that she was the minister's wife. She said that she had to get a lawyer in order to obtain information from my bank to get in touch with me because my bank manager refused to give her any information about me. She asked about her husband. I explained the whole situation to her. I explained to her that he left for India six days ago. She said that he lost his job some months ago and was very upset because he could not find work. She said that he withdrew a large sum of money from their account and left. I asked her if it was a custom for them to travel with money in their suitcase. She said yes. I asked her if he had his daughter's picture in his suitcase. She said yes. That verified what he told me. He even showed me the receipts he had from a hotel in California where he stayed before he came to New York. To my surprise, the woman phoned me the next day accusing me of her husband withdrawing the money from their account and is living with me. She said that she went to the bank to pay the mortgage and the money was not there. I again explained to her that her husband received the money which was transferred to my account and that he went to India. Since she did not believe me, I asked her please do not call me again. My Pastor often told the congregation that there were two missionary homes within the church: my home and another missionary who now lives in the Dominican Republic.

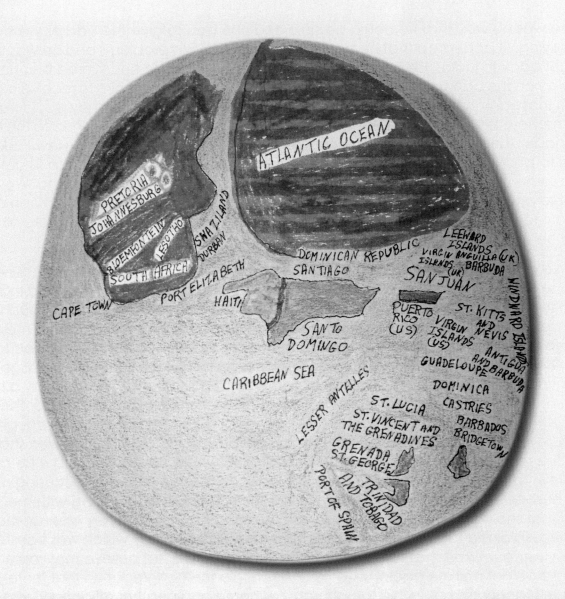

MY MISSION TO THE DOMINICAN REPUBLIC

The first missionary whose name was Missionary Williams who travelled to Barbados with my two children, Lucille, Walter, and me, said that she was born in the Dominican Republic. She wanted to learn about the mission field so she could return to the Dominican Republic to do missionary work. When she was preparing to go to the Dominican Republic, she asked some other members of the church which she was attending in New York City, as well as me, to go with her. The first time she went to the Dominican Republic, two missionaries accompanied her. It was Missionary Johnson and me. I had prayed and asked God for direction whether or not I should go. In a vision God took me to a place where I never went before. I was in a certain area with green shrubs. I also saw two little girls about nine years old and a little boy about three years old. God let me know that it was O.K. for me to go to the Dominican Republic. After making preparation, I accompanied the two missionaries on the trip. After arriving in the Dominican Republic, I was able to identify the place which I saw in the vision and also identify the two little girls who were twins, and the little boy. As soon as I saw them, I recognized them.

As missionaries, we visited the sick in the communities in their own homes, and witnessed to them. There were many hills and mountains to climb in order to reach the people. Some of the missionaries who lived there were given money and were asked to buy groceries and to cook food to take to the prison. Together we all visited the men in the prison and took food for them. We visited some of the churches and delivered the word of God to them.

On the second trip to the Dominican Republic, an Elder from their church, Elder Brown, who had never been overseas on the mission field before, wanted to have the experience of traveling abroad. There were four missionaries who travelled there. We distributed Holy Bibles and tracks written in the Spanish language, and also distributed clothing. The difference there was it is a Spanish speaking country. When I brought forth the word of God in English, the Spanish speaking missionary, in the group did the translation in Spanish for those who did not speak or understand English. When people spoke in Spanish, the same missionary translated in English to those who did not speak or understand Spanish. In the Dominican Republic, after climbing up the mountains, you then had to go down into the valley in order to reach the people or to get to the church. No vehicle could take you there. You had to walk.

There was no running water in the homes neither was there any toilets with running water. Some homes had no toilets at all. If you had to use the bathroom, you had to find a place outdoors as private as you could, and stoop down and do whatever you had to do. Sometimes in a home, the woman in the home may give you a pail to use so you did not have to go outdoors. Some people who only lived in America, in the city, never experienced that way of life, so it was difficult for them. Some may only have experienced using an outhouse, which is the same as an outdoor toilet without water. If they went to a camp in the country and the water toilets broke down, then they had to use an outhouse. For someone who had experienced that lifestyle before, they were still uncomfortable with the situation. What everyone had to remember was, "They were all on the mission field." That may have been the normal way of living for some of those people."

If the missionaries were invited to a family's house for dinner, the family would set the only table they had to accommodate the missionaries. They themselves would eat outdoors on the ground because it was not enough space at the table for them. While we, as missionaries appreciated the hospitality of the family, we humbled ourselves and decided to eat outdoors in the yard with the family.

It is very important when you travel on the mission field that you stay humble and not present yourself as highly uplifted above the people whom you are visiting. We all left the Dominican Republic and returned to America.

OTHER VISIONS

God gave me other visions while in the Dominican Republic. First he showed me that I needed to go to London to visit my best friend, Marva. I turned to the missionaries who were with me and told them that the Lord wanted me to go to London, England, when I returned to New York City. In the first vision God showed me that my best friend was on a large ship on the deep waters. Instead of it being clear water, there was much trash in the water that was left over on the ground, after the sugar canes in the fields had been reaped. In the mean time her sister, Gloria, as well as I, were walking up a stream of fresh clear water bare feet, wading in the water. I could not understand why the water was running up the hill instead of running down the hill.

MY MISSIONARY TRIP TO LONDON, ENGLAND

After returning to New York City, I prepared to go to London. Two of the missionaries went along with my daughter, Laurianne and me. When we arrived in London, we stayed with my best friend, her husband, and their two children. On the Sunday morning we visited a church with my best friend, Marva. During the service we took Holy Communion together. After the service was over, Marva and the two missionaries were aside talking. When I inquired what was going on, Marva said that she was telling the missionaries how she and I were confirmed together in Barbados and that we took our first Holy Communion together. She said that since she went to London, she had to work and care for her children. She sent them to church and Sunday school but she never went. She said that since we as missionaries came to London and we went to church together, she was happy because we came. It caused her to be in church that Sunday. She further went on to say that she and I stood side by side once again, receiving Holy Communion together there in London. That made her very happy.

MY MISSION TO ANTIGUA, WEST INDIES

My ministry also reached Antigua and Trinidad. In another vision, I was led to take my son, Walter, to Antigua, West Indies. I had visited there two times before with my first husband and met some of his family. My husband died many years later after the birth of our son Walter. I remembered some of the family's addresses. I wrote to two of them to let them know what the Lord was leading me to do. I received a response from one of them inviting me and my son to come and stay with them. They lived in Sea View Farm near a Methodist Church where my husband was born and brought up. I visited there and attended the church services with him many years ago, while on our honeymoon. Our son was born soon after we returned to New York City.

When we arrived in `Antigua, we went to the home of one of his cousins. There was an old lady about 84 years of age who told me that she was praying and asking God please let her live to see her cousin Joseph's son before she died. She was speaking of my son, Walter. She was also going blind. She thanked God for sending me to Antigua with my son. She prayed for us and blessed us as she said, "This is my Cousin Joseph's son."

It was Thanksgiving Day that year when Missionary Williams joined us. We all attended the church together with the family. We were introduced to the pastor of the church. There was a week of revival and Missionary Williams was asked to speak one night. During the day we were invited to have dinner with the pastor and his family. We were also invited to visit a hospital and nursing home there. We spoke with some of the doctors and nurses there and we prayed for the sick.

After returning to New York City, we attended the Holy Annual Convocation in Baltimore, Marilyn at our headquarter church. One of the brothers came and spoke to me. He asked me if I remembered him. I said that I did not know him. He identified himself as one of the young brothers who lived in the village of Sea View Farm in Antigua. He said that he was present at the church when the missionaries visited from New York City. He further went on to say that the visit was a blessing and that it was needed. He stated that the older members of their church wanted everything their way and did not include any room for the young people. He said that the young people were about to backslide because it was nothing for them to do in the church. After hearing the messages that were brought forth, it encouraged them to continue on worshipping God. You never know why God send you on the mission field. This young brother with his wife and their two children, a girl and a boy, had relatives living in the Bronx in New York City. They all went to New York to visit their relatives who were members of the Pentecostal Church which was affiliated with the Baltimore branch. Since their Holy Annual Convocation was going on, they were also invited to go along. That is how they ended up in Baltimore, Marilyn. We were all happy to see each other. They all enjoyed the services. That was around November that year.

During the summer months of July and August the next year, the camp season opened up in the Catskill Mountains. I volunteered as a counselor that year. Once again I met with the brother from Antigua, his wife, and their two children. Usually busses from each church in different states came up to the camp for baptism on the second Sunday in the month of July. They had a church service and Holy Communion before baptism. After baptism all of the people sat around at tables or on the ground to eat. They played games until about 4:30 P.M. All of the adults, except for those who were volunteering as counselors, or as kitchen staff for the camp season, and the children who were staying at camp, boarded their bus and went home. The two children from Antigua stayed at the camp for about two weeks. I became more acquainted with them. We, as missionaries, have to be able to recognize the voice of God when He speaks to us, and answer to his call. We must be obedient and do His Will at the time he wants us to.

THE MISSION TO TRINIDAD, WEST INDIES

On the mission to Trinidad, West Indies, I visited and stayed with a cousin of mine in the city of, "Maraval." I had with me, my younger daughter, Laurianne and my oldest grandson, Michael. We visited the church where she worshipped. We all attended Sunday School and worship service. There were many children in attendance.

The clothing which I took to Trinidad had to be distributed from my cousin's home. My cousin Coreen said that the pastor of the church could not distribute the clothing and foodstuff from the church because the people would keep coming, expecting to receive clothing and foodstuff when he did not have anything else to give. I discovered that people in the community often came to her house when they had nothing to cook for their children, expecting her to help them. She often shared with them whatever she had. During a conversation with my cousin Coreen, I was also informed that one girl continually collapsed in school. She was taken to the doctor who informed the mother that the child needed nourishment. Her mother had nothing to feed her before she went to school. I was reminded that there are people in the world who don't have food to eat.

THE MISSION TO GRENADA, WEST INDIES

A few years later, the pastor of my church, Pastor Jones, accompanied my younger daughter, Laurianne and me to Barbados and Grenada. She said that God instructed her in a vision to go to Barbados and Grenada. We visited churches in Barbados before going to Grenada. One of the pastors in Barbados, Pastor Green, was affiliated with the church in Grenada. He had visited our church in New York City. He went ahead of us to Grenada. He took with him, the clothes which we brought with us from New York City, to be distributed to the people there. When we arrived in Grenada, we visited the nursing home there. In walking up the hill to the nursing home, we saw a soldier with a long revolver guarding a building. With curiosity, I asked the soldier, "If I try to enter that building, would you shoot me?" The soldier responded, "Yes I would." We never knew that a war was brewing there. We spent three days in Grenada and returned to Barbados on the third day. While in Grenada, the message that God brought forth through me, was for the people of the church in Grenada to stay covered under the blood of Jesus so that if anything developed, they would be safe under the blood of Jesus.

We stayed three more days in Barbados before returning to New York City. Laurianne did not want to return to New York City. She begged me to let her stay in Barbados. When I asked her why she did not want to return to New York City, she said that it was too noisy. She complained about the noise from the fire trucks and all of the shooting that she experienced. After checking with my relatives where we were staying, I inquired from my cousin, Mary, if she would take the responsibility of caring for

Laurianne if I left her in Barbados. She informed me that she would. I then asked her what was the procedure of Laurianne staying and going to school in Barbados. I was told that I had to check with the Barbados Embassy. After checking and receiving the information, the necessary papers were filled out. My cousin, Mary, who was a school mistress at one of the schools there, took the responsibility of registering her for school. She also took the responsibility of getting uniforms made for her.

After returning to New York City, I went to church that Sunday morning. I was approached by one of our ministers who asked me if I knew that there was a war in Grenada. I told her that there was no war in Grenada that we just left there. Later on that day, we discovered from the radio broadcast that a war did break out and that no one was allowed to enter or leave Grenada. It was called, "The American Invasion of The Caribbean Island of Grenada." Knowing that Barbados was near to Grenada, we were concerned about Laurianne's safety. I was told to contact the American Embassy and inform them that my daughter, who was an American Citizen, was in Barbados and that we were concerned for her safety because of the war in Grenada. In doing so, I was informed that she was safe.

I thought of the fact that, when my pastor told me that God was sending her on a mission to Barbados and Grenada, I told her that I did not have any money to travel overseas. She told me that it would not make any sense for her to go to Barbados which is my home and I was not going. My daughter, Laurianne, was seven years old and I would have to find someone to care for her when I was gone. I prayed that night about the situation before going to bed. When I awoke the next morning, I phoned my Pastor to tell her what happened during the night. I told her that I had a dream. In the dream I heard the voice of God asking me, "Did I not send you on the mission field before when you did not have money?" I answered, "Yes Lord." He then asked me, "Did I not make the way clear for you so you could go?" I answered "Yes Lord." I told my Pastor that I woke up repenting and telling God how sorry I was and asked Him please to forgive me. I then told the Lord "Yes Lord, I will go on the mission field with my Pastor to Barbados and Grenada." All of this happened during the week.

About two Sundays later while at church, after the service was dismissed, one of the sisters of the church walked up to me, put her arm around my shoulders as both of us walked the floor. The sister said to me, "Your way has been paid to Barbados and Grenada." When I asked who paid it? I was told, "Never you mind. It has already been paid." I thanked God it was paid. As my Pastor began to make the preparations for the mission, I gathered up enough money to pay the plane fare for my daughter. I wrote to one of my cousins in Barbados explaining the situation and asked if we could stay with her. My cousin agreed. When we arrived in Barbados, I contacted the Pastor there, Pastor Green, who had visited our church in New York City. He made arrangements for us to visit different churches in Barbados. After discussing with him how God was leading, and how we brought clothes for the people at the church which he was affiliated with in Grenada, he made arrangements to take the clothes to Grenada ahead of us. He would also let the Pastor there know that we were coming to Grenada. The Pastor of Grenada, Pastor Brice, in turn made provisions for us to stay at her home. Her living quarters was up stairs over where they held their services.

Pastor Brice gave up both of her bedrooms and her beds. One she gave to my Pastor from New York City, Pastor Jones, and the other for my daughter Laurianne and me.

Sometime during the night, my Pastor, Pastor Jones, discovered that Pastor Brice was sleeping on the floor with her children. She came to the bedroom where my daughter and me were sleeping, and informed me of what was happening. She said that we did not come to Grenada to inconvenience Pastor Brice and her family. While we were grateful that she made the sacrifice to accommodate us, we did not want her sleeping on the floor. We gave one of her bedrooms back to her.

The following morning when everyone awoke and were about to take a bath, we discovered that the pipe was not giving any water. The only way to take a bath was to walk down the hill to the beach and take a bath in the ocean. Since we were not prepared for the beach, we had to bathe in a dress. That was the norm for the people there. If the pipe was giving water, the people from the neighborhood gathered at her house, in the backyard, and took turns bathing under her pipe. I was familiar with some of these experiences from my childhood but I did not know that such conditions still existed.

I have said all of this to let you, as readers know, when you feel or hear the calling of God in your lives and His anointing upon you, please answer to his call. Be obedient to what he has called you to do. If you do not understand, seek help from your spiritual leaders. I realized that God had called the mission to Barbados and Grenada. He sent us there to deliver a message to the people of Grenada, and brought us out safely before the war broke out. We thanked God for sending us on the mission on time, and bringing us home safely. During the news broadcast about the war, we realized that the nursing home where we visited the senior citizens was one of the first places to be destroyed. Just think of all of those senior citizens having to spend the last days of their lives in a nursing home and the nursing home being destroyed and their lives suddenly comes to an end. That was another part of the missionary journey.

ANOTHER TRIP TO BARBADOS

On several occasions, I returned to Barbados continuing my missionary work. I did not realize that I needed to receive updated papers for my land since the government cut off two portions of it. The draftsman, whom I asked to draw the plan, informed me that he could not draw a plan to build the house and conference room / mission, unless he had the correct measurement and boundaries of the land. That was another delay. After contacting the land tax department again, one of their employees said to me, "you have been coming up here for many years with the same problem and no one is doing anything to help you. I am going to make it my business to help you." With that being said, the worker went to her office and began making phone calls to different departments informing them of the problems that I was having. The worker was given the phone numbers to different departments. She kept dialing the numbers until she reached the right person to get the information which she needed. After obtaining the correct information, she was told that I needed to get in touch with a land survey who would measure the land for me. Since she discovered that the government's land surveyor had measured and cut off the land, which the government needed, all he had to do was to go into the computer and print out the correct measurement of land that was left. She gave me the number to contact him. After making several attempts, I was soon able to contact him and explain what I needed from him.

A few weeks later, I received the new papers showing the correct measurement and boundaries of my portion of land. It was then that the draftsman was able to draw the plans for the house and conference room. This had to be filed with the Town and Country Planning for its approval. I discussed with the draftsman what the conference room was going to be used for. He registered the drawing as a private residence with a prayer room. The government approved it with a prayer room.

The next step was to find a builder or a contractor to start the project. Since the death of my husband in March 2008, I realized that he spoke with me on the Sunday night of February 10, 2008, before going to sleep. When I woke up the Monday morning, February 11, 2008, I discovered that he took sick during the night. He fell in the room onto the floor. He did not speak one word since that Sunday night. The doctors said that he had a massive stroke and a heart attack. I realized that I no longer had my husband to assist me in the planning to build the house and conference room as he was doing before. I sought help from different people to find a builder.

During my vacation and retirement celebration in Barbados in August 2007, one of my prayer partners, a teacher, who also worked with me in New York City, was also on vacation. We, with my next-door neighbors, also celebrated my late husband's birthday.

In visiting the land, he introduced me to several people whom he realized were related to him. One of them was able to locate the correct person to draw the plans for the house and prayer room. I would then need help in hiring a contractor or a builder. No one knew that God was going to take him home early the next year. I did not want the same thing to happen to me where I could not speak. I would then be unable to give instructions of how I believed God wanted me to build the prayer room. At that time, the doctors were saying that there were so many things wrong with me, it seemed that I would die at any time soon. I was introduced to a builder around March 2009. I informed him of my plans and I gave him a copy of the drawing for the building. He assured me that he could do the job and that I did not need a contractor. Soon after that, a large sum of money was deposited on a bank to pay as a deposit to the builder to start building the house and prayer room. I explained to him that the prayer room had to be built first. He explained to me that all of the foundation had to be built first before the prayer room could be erected. I returned to New York City, leaving someone to check on the work as the builder did the ground breaking and started the work in March 2010.

While in New York City, I continued my missionary work. I also checked back with the builder to see how the work was progressing. Many times I requested a contract from the builder but he kept making excuses. He projected himself to be honest for some time but then he changed. Maybe it should be said that his true character serviced after I continued to request a contract and questioned how the money was being spent. He kept making excuses and promised that when the building got to a certain point he would give me a contract but he never did. My greatest mistake was starting the work without a contract. When the structure of the prayer room was up, he was paid another large sum of money to buy certain materials and pay a well digger to dig two wells. He came back the next day and asked for another six hundred dollars ($600.00) to build a cover for the well. He knew that I was scheduled to leave the next day for New York City. I gave him that sum of money. I requested a receipt from him. Since I was leaving for New York, I asked him to give the receipt to my daughter. He never gave her the receipt but asked her for more money after I left. He had the well diggers start the well before I left but then made excuse that the soil was wet so they could not complete it. I felt that when the soil was dry he would let them continue and complete the well so that the plumber could install the pipes and the toilets.

While I was in New York City, he phoned me asking for more money. When I asked him what was done with the money he already had, he said that he did something else with it. He never said what he did with it. When I returned to Barbados, the well still was not completed. I saw the well digger on the premises. He informed me that he kept asking the builder, when will he allow him to finish digging the well. He said that the builder told him that I went back to New York and did not leave money to finish the well. I told him that I gave the builder a check before I left to pay for the well, and to have the electrical work completed in the small room. When I returned to Barbados, I discovered that none of that work was done. Of the extra money I sent him, he still did not complete the wells or the small room. He claimed that he bought paint and painted the prayer room. I did not request the prayer room to be painted at that time. That was the last thing to be done, when all the other work was completed. He did work which he wanted to do so he could be paid rather than paying other people to do the work which I requested to be done. He knew that I wanted the prayer room painted in gold but he painted it in off white. It cost me more money to hire someone else to paint it the way I wanted it done. He also painted the kitchen before the counter was built. After building the counter, all of that paint was wasted because it was all messed up with the cement. The money which he took for his salary and also for the mason was a total lost for me.

After receiving another check to purchase more materials and to pay the workers, he told me that the plumber and the electrician said that if I did not pay them one thousand dollars each by that Friday, they will not be working for me any longer. I told him that I just gave him a check for four thousand dollars ($4,000.00) and that he should pay them out of that. He said that he does not do business like that. He refused to pay the workers, telling them that I had to pay them. He took the check and left. The attendance book which he kept had no information on the workers, just their names and how much he paid them each week. He said that he no longer wanted to work for me. When I took the keys from him, I requested the names and phone numbers of the plumber and the electrician. He gave them to me. When I phoned them to inquire if they would continue to work for me, I learned that they were never paid for their work for over one year because the builder told them that I was to pay them. He hired them when they were needed. He gave me an estimate of the cost of the materials they each needed and the cost of their wages. I paid him the money including their wages. When I checked the attendance book which I had from the builder, their names were not even recorded in the book to show when they worked. They both said that they worked for over a year and one only received six hundred ($600.00) and the other only received four hundred dollars ($400.00). That was money which they spent for materials and was being reimbursed. I was much surprised that I visited the job site on many occasions with them being present and they never uttered one word that they were not being paid. He had the workers separated so they would not talk to me or answer any questions which I asked them. He boasted about the houses he built for other people. What I found out was, their were men in charge of the work who would not pay him until they were satisfied with the work. I felt that he took advantage of me because he knew that I am a widow and a senior citizen. The person who was checking the work for me was also a senior citizen and the builder did not want to speak with him when questions arose. I had to take the keys back from him and then pay someone else to continue the work. I hope that this information will help to make you aware of things that could happen to you if you have to build a mission. Always seek directions from God first and be sure that you are working in the time that he requires for you to do the work. Also make sure that you have a written contract signed by the contractor and yourself. If possible, have a witness.

VOLUNTEERING IN THE PRISON MINISTRY IN NEW YORK CITY AND STATE

After returning to New York City, I continued my missionary work visiting the hospital prison at the Belleview Hospital and the prison in Up State New York. The hospital prison consisted of prisoners who were sick in prison and were transferred to the Belleview Hospital Prison wards for medical treatment. The inmates were encouraged to assemble in the recreation room for worship service with the visiting missionaries and ministers. During the service, the inmates were encouraged to participate by choosing to sing a song or hymn they knew, or to give a testimony. The service sometimes lasted for at least 30 or 45 minutes. Sometimes they were allowed to ask questions if they were not being disruptive.

In order to get into the prison area, you had to show a special ID. A security officer would check your ID against a list they kept on file to see if you were scheduled to attend service that day. If you were, the second gate would be opened to let you in. Then that gate was locked. You would be escorted to a room where you were required to leave your coat and any bags you had. Ladies must remove any hat pins from their hats. You were only allowed to take your Bible and any religious tracks or extra Bibles you may have to distribute to the inmates. The missionaries always prayed before visiting the prison wards.

In visiting the prison up State New York, you were also required to lock up your coat and pocket book. You were not allowed to take your Bible or any written materials such as news papers or magazines into the visiting area. Since you may be visiting an individual whom you know, you were allowed to take a food package mostly of canned foods weighing no more than 35 pounds once per month. One can of food is only expected to weigh 16 ounces or less. You were given large brown paper bags to put the groceries in with the name and address of the person written on it. You had to itemize everything you had in each bag and write how many ounces in each can. This list was given in at the reception desk with the bags of groceries. When your name was called to visit the inmate, you were then escorted to another building.

The most humiliating experience that I had to go through was to be told that I must go to a bathroom with a male security officer standing in front of the bathroom door. He gave me a brown paper bag and told me to take off my brazier and place it in the bag. He instructed me to give him the bag with my brazier in it as I exit the bath room. Then I was directed to go through the scanner, return to the security guard, and collect my brazier from him. I was again instructed to go into a different bathroom to put back on my brazier before going through another area to visit the inmate. The first time I had that experience, my husband and older daughter, Lucille, were with me. The second time my husband had died and Lucille was again with me. I cried and cried. The security officer asked Lucille what was wrong with me. To him it seemed as though it was a normal thing for a woman to take off her brazier in a public bathroom without any shame and hand it to a stranger who was a man. I was not used to that. There are many humiliating moments that missionaries go through sometimes, in order to win souls to Christ.

LIVING THE PRAYER OF JABEZ

One of my sisters, Naomi, had introduced my husband and me to a book titled, "The Prayer of Jabez." As I read the book, I began to pray, "The Prayer of Jabez," for myself, asking God to extend my territory. I never knew that God would extend my territory as far as Johannesburg, Cape Town, and Soweto, in South Africa to do missionary work there with my daughter Laurianne, and other missionaries from other churches. I never thought that I would have the privilege of visiting Robin Island and enter the prison cell where the former and late South African President Mandela was kept in prison for many years, according to history. I never knew that I would have been able to visit churches in North Carolina and Miami, Florida. These are places I always wanted to go. I told people many times, be careful what you pray and ask God for. He may give it to you but not in the way you expect it.

THE MISSIONARY JOURNEY TO SOUTH AFRICA

On February 12, 2010, a group of ten missionaries including a pastor, my daughter, Laurianne, and me gathered together at the J.F. Kennedy International Airport in New York City. We all boarded the South African Airline on a flight leaving for Johannesburg, South Africa. We were all on a mission to help as many people in different parts of South Africa as we could. The flight took about 18 hours. After arriving in Johannesburg, South Africa, we were met at the airport by a bus driver who identified himself as the tour guide for our group. He took us to the Michael Angelo Hotel where we were later joined with another group of pastors and other leaders from different states in the United States of America. After having dinner, some of the group went sightseeing in the neighborhood. Some of them even went to the Safari. We later met and reviewed the agenda for the next day.

The next morning after breakfast, everyone boarded the tour bus and we headed for different parts of Johannesburg. We had lunch at a restaurant. At the end of that day we returned to the hotel. The next day after breakfast, we went to Soweto. There we visited the home where the former and late President Mandela of South Africa once lived. It is now a museum. We later had dinner and settled down at the hotel in Cape Town where we could see the Table Top Mountain. Table Top Mountain is a mountain that has a flat top with the shape of a rectangle. On a windy day, the clouds hang down over it, making it look like a table with a table cloth on it.

Another day we went on a tour to Robin Island where the former and late President Mandela was imprisoned for many years. The tour guide pointed out to the group the difference in the neighborhoods as we travelled the highway and the little country roads. We saw people washing their clothes by the side of the road at the stand pipe. We saw the type of houses that the poor people live in. They call them shanty houses. We were told that most of these people walked about and picked up whatever scraps of wood they found in order to build shacks for them and their family to live in. They also weaved the branches from the coconut palm trees to help make a roof for their shack to keep the rain and the sun out. Some people were also seen by the side of the road with a tray selling fruits, drinks, and candy. In another area lived the rich people in their fancy houses built of wall. The color of the soil was gold from the gold dust in the mines.

The tour guide also took us to another area where we met at a certain church with other missionaries who lived in South Africa. There, some of the missionaries were assigned to lead song service, and pray for the people. Some counseled the women in different areas of their lives, some worked with the children, and some were assigned to distribute the clothing and foodstuff. They also distributed toiletries for the adults and books for the children. Because I love and care for children, I chose to work with the children. For me, that meant having wipes for them to clean their faces and hands and having snacks to give them. I also took games, books, and toys of my own, to work with the children. I really enjoyed that trip. I thought of being hungry as a child and having people in my community to be concerned enough about me to feed me and then send food home by me so that my mother would have food to feed my other siblings. At the end of the day, the books and toys were given to the children to take home. Both the children and their parents were appreciative.

Tickets with numbers for about four hundred families were given out in order for the families to collect the bags of food, clothing, and other health items. When everything was distributed, people were still coming. There was still a long line of people but nothing was left to give them. It was quite an experience. I began reflecting on my life as a child in Barbados. Many times my mother sent me to different family members who worked in the plantation at Fairy Valley to ask them for something to cook to feed her children. I also thought of the school mistress who never thought that any of her students would ever make it to America or any place overseas. The school mistress even said to one girl whose mother was in America, that if the girl ever got to America, the only job she would ever get was to wash dishes, scrub floors, and scrub the side of the walls. I wondered what would the school mistress have said, if she was still alive today, knowing that my daughter and me were able to visit South Africa, "The Mother Land," where our ancestors came from.

What I thought of most of all was the fact that my mother, sending me to other family members' homes to ask for something to cook, was actually training me to become a missionary. I developed the habit of being concerned about the needs of other people and the desire to help them. My late husband, Elder E. Clarke, often told me, "Baby Doll, you cannot solve the world's problems."

As the group of us as missionaries entered a restaurant to have lunch, the tradition of those who worked in the restaurant was to make sure that your hands were clean before you entered the door. One or two of the restaurant workers greeted you at the door with containers of water and a hand towel for each individual. They poured the water on each individual's hands with a little soap and handed to each individual a clean hand towel to dry their hands. Then someone else escorted you to your seats. There was an area for the buffet and each group from the table was directed to select their food. If it was a dish that any of us were not familiar with, one of the workers would explain what the food was.

While we were eating, there was a group of children who came into the restaurant to entertain us. They sang a few songs and did a performance. That was their way of earning money to help themselves. The restaurant owner permitted it so they encouraged us to give the children a donation. Even though we were on the mission field, we were still learning about our own cultural background.

The people of South Africa welcomed each one of us as we walked through the different neighborhoods by saying, "Welcome home." They identified us as their own people who were taken away from their country many years ago during slavery. We were able to visit many historical places including the school where many school children were murdered during a demonstration many years ago. The pictures are displayed in paintings on the school premises and also in a museum near the school with the history of what happened that day at their school. Some art work is also carved on the ground around the school. One thing you must remember when traveling, always stay with your group. Never wander off alone. It is for your safety.

In order to bring part of the experience of being in South Africa back to the church, we bought a CD with some of the songs the Africans sang in the Zulu language as they worshipped and gave praise to God. My daughter, Laurianne, translated one of the songs into the English language. During a Sunday morning service when missionaries were in charge, I requested the musician to play the CD of the song, "Jylo," while an usher held up the translation of the words in English for the congregation to read, as I explained our experience while in South Africa. My Pastor said that it was a good experience for the congregation. They sang the song in the Zulu language and then in the English language. Since then, I have heard other songs sung in our church which we heard and sang for the first time in South Africa.

THE RETURN TRIP TO NEW YORK CITY AND THE TRIP TO HAWAII

After returning to New York City from South Africa, I was escorted to Hawaii by my son, Walter, for about two weeks. He knew that I always wanted to go to Hawaii. Since he was on vacation, he decided to take me there. He felt that I worked hard all of my life and that now I am retired, I should be able to travel and visit the places I always wanted to visit. That was a different journey. We were both able to tour two major war ships that were used when the bomb was dropped on Eroshima. On the first ship which was named, "The Battle Ship Missouri," the tour guide explained to us how they called it, "The Mighty Mo. He said that during World War 11, when the soldiers died, there was no way to preserve their bodies or return them to their countries or to their parents. They just placed the soldiers' bodies in body bags and threw them overboard in the sea. Oh how my heart hurt as I heard such a story. I remembered my childhood days in St. Bartholomew's Church when the priest, in his prayers, said to remember the soldiers who are gone to war. I remembered the congregation singing a hymn with the words, "for those in peril on the sea." I thought of the parents whose sons went to war and they never heard from them and never saw them again. I thought of how painful it was for them.

The second ship, "The USS Arizona," was just buried under the water. They could not raise it up neither could they save any of the soldiers. They were just buried in the ship in the ocean. A museum was built over the sunken ship. We had to take a ship to visit the museum. A list of all of the names of those who perished on the ship was written in the museum. You can still see the remains of the buried ship under the water.

My son and I were also able to visit the Polynesian Cultural Arts and Craft Center. In some of the things which I saw was the old traditional way of cooking in a pit. They dug a pit, lit the fire, wrapped the food in banana leaves, placed it into the pit and then covered it with the fire. The heat cooked the food. We also visited a headquarter church whose leadership we were told sponsored the Polynesian students to do their cultural display. They were being trained as missionaries. They went to school on scholarships and worked in their spare time to help support themselves.

As I continued my visits to Barbados, I kept working on completing the vision. I am hoping and praying that God will bless me with the finances needed to complete and dedicate the prayer room in the year 2014 to be used for the glory and honor of God.

As I continue with the polishing up of the Prayer room, my friends and prayer partners in New York City are excited about it and are looking forward to participating in the dedication service. I hope that in the future, I will be able, through donations, to present food baskets to the sick and shut in especially at Christmas time. I also would like to contribute to assisting missionaries and young children who desire the experience to travel abroad on the mission field.

Many years ago during my missionary work, I sponsored a little girl, about nine years of age from Barbados, and gave her the opportunity to experience life in America for a summer vacation. She was also given the experience of spending at least two weeks at a sleep away camp in the Catskill Mountains with other children from different cultural backgrounds. About a year later, I assisted in sponsoring a little boy, about seven years old from my church assembly in New York City, and brought him to Barbados for two weeks vacation, to experience life in Barbados. This also gave his parents a break so they could enjoy their summer vacation. Because of these examples, many other children from the church assembly were taken to the Dominican Republic to experience life there in a Spanish culture.

Most recently in the year 2010, I was led to sponsor a mother and her two young children for three weeks vacation, to experience life in New York City. When her four year old daughter saw the different school supplies in the stores, all she talked about was taking things back to Barbados for her teacher. When they returned to Barbados, her daughter returned to her school in September. She told her teacher of her vacation in New York City. She drew a picture of the tall buildings she saw and then drew a picture of Mrs. Clarke, as she calls me. When the teacher asked her to tell about the picture, she described the drawing which looked like a water bug, as Mrs. Clarke. When her mother picked her up from school, her teacher told her mother what her daughter did. Her mother looked at the picture and asked her daughter if Mrs. Clarke was a cockroach. The daughter said no. Her mother showed the picture to me, as I was visiting Barbados at that time. I also said that the picture looked like a large cockroach/ water bug. While at school the next day the child drew her second picture. It represented the same Mrs. Clarke. It still looked like a cockroach/ water bug. To the adults this seemed funny. I asked the child, "Why did you draw Mrs. Clarke as a cockroach?" The child replied, "It is not a cockroach. It is a lady bug." I asked her to please describe the cockroach and then the ladybug. I then asked her to tell the difference between the two. She said that the cockroach was all one color, black, but the lady bug, even though it was black, it had beautiful red spots on it. In other words, I had to apologize to her for misinterpreting her picture. We can still learn much from children.

Recently I came across a letter dated 1998, addressed to me from a grandmother who accompanied her granddaughter on a visit to America. I had sponsored the grand-daughter and her mother, who was the sister of my husband to spend a summer vacation in New York City with my husband and me. Since her mother was not granted a visa to accompany her, the grandmother came with the child at a later date. In the letter, the grandmother was thanking me for giving her the opportunity to visit New York City. She mentioned the fun they had. She also mentioned how they were walking the street when she did not recognize that on the same level she walked onto the South Ferry boat. When the boat started off in the water to go to Staten Island, the grandmother thought she was still on land. When I asked her to look up after taking her seat, she realized that she was on the boat on the water. She was much surprised. When the captain sounded the horn of the boat, the grand-daughter jumped because it startled her. Everyone started laughing. One man asked the grand-daughter where she was going, if she was going to jump off the boat. On another day, we all went to Coney Island with my daughter, Laurianne. Everyone had fun. The grandmother and her granddaughter enjoyed their visit to New York City and loved shopping.

Throughout all of the missionary journeys, I realized that each one gave a different experience. The journey to South Africa presented itself as a most organized and financially planned trip.

We attended, "The International Women's Convention." It had been going on for many years. The people involved were able to plan way ahead of time for the expenses involved. They were able to charge the complete price for the trip which included the price to pay for hotels. Those leaders involved, set up a timely payment plan which allowed the participants to budget themselves in order to pay for the trip. Most local church trips may be just a vision given to an individual to visit their own country or a place where someone they knew came from. They may not have funds to pay for a hotel. Their church may not be in a position to help them financially. They may own their own home in that country or they may seek lodging from their friends or relatives to accommodate them or any guest that may be traveling with them on the mission field.

WHY THE NAME "GARDEN OF PRAYER?"

As the building was erected and almost completed, I was asked by my Pastor, "What is the name of your ministry?" My response to her was, it is the "Lumsby-Clarke Prayer Room." She said to me, "I do not mean the name of the prayer room, but the name of the ministry." I had not thought before of giving the ministry a name. All I thought of was doing what I believed God wanted me to do. My Pastor kept telling me that I needed to give the ministry a name. I told her that I would think about it. After thinking about it, I quickly remembered that I spent much time on that property when I was a teenager, praying and crying and asking God to help me. I was very unhappy and did not know what to do except to pray. I remembered that there were always beautiful pink flowers growing there on vines. I would pick some of the flowers and stick them in my hair. On the other side of my property was the family's land which grew all kinds of vegetables and fruits which I often picked and ate.

I remembered being pregnant out of wedlock and being classified as a disgrace to my family. As I walked on the pasture looking across at the horizon of the ocean, I thought of how dead bodies sometimes washed up on the seashore when I was living in Sea View as a little girl growing up. I thought of going to the sea to drown myself but it was too far to walk. I found myself lying on this same pasture in the heat of the midday sun, just wishing that I would get sick and die. I thought that life was not worth living. I began to question God and asked him why he did not let me die when I was in the hospital with my appendix burst at the age of fourteen years old. The doctors acted quickly to stop the poison from going throughout my body. Most people in that condition at that time did not live but God spared my life. Now I was asking God, why did He let me live. Somehow I remembered the scripture which read "Can the dead praise thee O God?" Psalm 88:10. I realized that if I was dead that I could not praise God. It was then that I realized I wanted to live to praise God. I did not remember any of this until my Pastor asked me for the name of my ministry. Then God brought back all of this to my memory. He also brought back to my memory the song, "I Come to the Garden Alone." "The Garden Of Prayer Mission," is built on the same spot. I realized that I must return to the same spot and give my testimony to the people here as well as whoever attends this dedication service. It is my hope to encourage people to, "PRAY WITHOUT CEASING." Pray when everything is going well and pray when things go wrong because, "Prayer changes things." It is my desire to leave this prayer room and the history of why it was built.

The Lumsby-Clarke Garden of Pray International Mission is a room set apart in my family home , and is dedicated as "A Peace Offering, To The Glory And Honor Of God." It will always carry the history of, "The Lumsby-Clarke Garden of Prayer Domestic and International Ministry." It may be used for prayer or retreats. It may also be used to accommodate missionaries traveling from abroad, if they so desire to stay here. Arrangements may be made through the persons in charge. "The Lumsby-Clarke Garden of Prayer International Ministry" is a legacy for my children, Walter N. Lumsby and Laurianne E. Lumsby, hoping that its history and the purpose for which the building is intended for will benefit them and whoever else participates in its ministry. All I ask for is that whoever is involved in the prayer ministry take great care of the building, treat it with respect, and use it for the purpose which it is intended for and let God bless you. Two other things I will say is, be truthful and honest in whatever you do, and, as an Elementary School Teacher said to me when I was in Class Four, in Barbados, "But Seek ye first the kingdom of God, and His righteousness; and all these things shall be added unto you." Matthew Chapter 6, verse 33 of The Holy Bible, King James Version.

ABOUT THE AUTHOR

As Author of her second book, Missionary Isabella L-Clarke wishes to convey some of the experiences which she encountered on the mission field to you, the reader. She hopes that it will help to prepare you as a missionary for the mission field. During her years of training as a missionary and working diligently on the mission field, she was ordained as an International Evangelist. As she continued to minister to, and supply the needs of many people domestically and internationally, she was also ordained as an Elder. Missionary Isabella L-Clarke was also a member of the organization, "The Association Aide for The Physically Handicapped Children of Barbados." She visited some of the homes, hospics, and school for the deaf. She continues her ministry through the church in which she is a member, and where she presently worships. She has been a guiding light to many people.

In the job where she worked as a teacher for over 22 years, some of her coworkers came to her in times of their difficulty in life and requested her to pray for them. Before her work day began, during her lunch break, and after her work day was ended, many people came to her requesting prayers. On Friday afternoons when work was ended, before they left for home, they met again in her classroom for prayer.

Since her retirement in July 2007, she has been attending meetings for "Retired Teachers." One day in June 2013, on her way to a meeting, she saw one of the male teachers whom she worked with. After greeting each other, he told her that she was the light that kept him working on the job. She was much surprised to hear that. She hopes that the information given will benefit you and that you may understand how important it is to listen to the voice of God, and obey His calling upon your life. She tries to give you the pictures of a mission being built from the foundation of the earth. When everything seemed to be going well, then problems developed. What do you do? Do you give up? No. You continue to pray, use what resources you still have, and allow God to bring you through, until the mission is completed.

Pictures of the building were taken by her daughter Laurianne. Pictures in her missionary uniform were saved from when her ministry first began.